W9-BSK-245

The Country
Dried Flower Companion

The Country
Dried Flower Companion

STEPHEN WOODHAMS

Photography by James Merrell

CollinsPublishersSanFrancisco
A Division of HarperCollins*Publishers*

THE COUNTRY DRIED FLOWERS COMPANION
Stephen Woodhams

First published in USA in 1995
by Collins Publishers San Francisco
1160 Battery Street, San Francisco CA 94111

First published in Great Britain in 1995 by Mitchell Beazley
an imprint of Reed Consumer Books Limited

Photography by *James Merrell*
Illustrations by *Michael Hill*

Art Editor *Trinity Fry*
Editors *Jennifer Jones & Jonathan Hilton*
Art Director *Jacqui Small*
Executive Editor *Judith More*
Production *Heather O'Connell*

Library of Congress Cataloging-in-Publication Data
Woodhams, Stephen.
The country dried flowers companion/Stephen Woodhams: photography by James Merrell.
  p. cm.
Includes index.
ISBN 0-00-255492-5
1. Dried flower arrangement.   I Title
SB449.3.D7W67   1995
745.92--dc20   94-42867
                                           CIP

The publishers have made every effort to ensure that all instructions given in this book are accurate and safe,
but they cannot accept liability for any resulting injury, damage or loss to either person or property,
whether direct or consequential and howsoever arising. The authors and publishers will be grateful
for any information which will assist them in keeping future editions up to date.

Colour reproduction by Rival Colour, UK
Produced by Mandarin Offset
Printed and bound in Hong Kong

contents

*M*Y OBJECTIVE IN WRITING THIS BOOK IS TO SHARE WITH YOU SOME OF THE MORE POPULAR COUNTRY-STYLE DESIGNS I HAVE DEVISED OVER THE YEARS. NOT EVERYBODY HAS THE SAME LEVEL OF EXPERTIZE OR, INDEED, THE TIME NECESSARY TO CREATE VERY ELABORATE DRIED-FLOWER ARRANGEMENTS, SO I HAVE ALSO INCLUDED SOME VERY SIMPLE BUT, NEVERTHELESS, EFFECTIVE COMPOSITIONS. WHEREVER POSSIBLE, YOU WILL FIND SUGGESTED LOCATIONS IN THE HOME FOR THE ARRANGEMENTS, BUT HALF THE FUN IS TRYING OUT

NEW AND UNUSUAL PLACINGS, SO THE BEST ADVICE ON THIS POINT IS

ALWAYS TO FOLLOW YOUR INSTINCTS. FOR EASY REFERENCE, MOST OF

THE DRIED-FLOWER ARRANGEMENTS HAVE BEEN GROUPED BY COLOR,

SO IF YOU ARE PLANNING TO DECORATE A PARTICULAR ROOM OR CRE-

ATING A SPECIAL SCHEME YOU SHOULD BE ABLE TO FIND A SUITABLE

DESIGN QUITE EASILY. I HAVE ALSO INCLUDED A SELECTION OF MY DE-

SIGNS THAT ARE PARTICULARLY FRAGRANT OR ARE SUITABLE FOR A

SPECIFIC SEASON OR IMPORTANT FAMILY EVENT.

introduction

Materials

*a*NY CRAFT IS EASIER TO LEARN IF YOU HAVE A BASIC KIT OF GOOD-QUALITY TOOLS AND MATERIALS. FOR DRIED FLOWERS, YOU NEED VERY LITTLE IN THIS REGARD — SCISSORS AND SECATEURS, 6 AND 12IN (15 AND 30CM) STUB WIRES, BLACK REEL TAPE, STRING, RAFFIA, AND A TAPE MEASURE. AS IMPORTANT AS THE FLOWERS IN MAKING AN ARRANGEMENT IS THE CONTAINER IN WHICH YOU DISPLAY IT. A CONTAINER HELPS TO DETERMINE THE HEIGHT AND SPREAD OF A DISPLAY, AND LENDS IT THE IMPORTANT ATTRIBUTES OF SHAPE, TEXTURE, COLOR, AND ARCHITECTURAL FORM. NOWADAYS, THERE IS SO MUCH CHOICE — FROM TRADITIONAL VASES, WICKER BASKETS, AND TERRA COTTA POTS TO MORE UNUSUAL CONTAINERS SUCH AS COAL SCUTTLES, TEA POTS, FOOTBATHS, AND METAL BUCKETS.

materials

ABOVE *A good selection of the constructional elements required for some arrangements.*
BELOW *Natural materials, such as shells, cones and twigs are always useful ingredients.*
OPPOSITE *Flowers that are typically available.*

The more materials you have to choose from the better when creating a dried-flower arrangement. Gather together a variety of different raffias – natural and colored – string and rope of different weights and textures, plaited grasses, cinnamon sticks, dried florist's foam, a selection of mosses – such as lichen, carpet and sphagnum – stub wires and reel wire. Glue may be useful, too.

Also important for their design qualities are different types of sea shell, pebbles, driftwood, bundles of twigs, nuts, dried berries and fir cones. Keep these materials neatly in glass jars and you will be able to view all of your potential "ingredients" at a glance if looking for inspiration. You might want an arrangement that features a particular texture or combination of contrasting textures, one centered around a color theme or one relevant to the room in which it will be seen.

If planning a dried arrangement for a kitchen, for example, you might tend toward wheat and herbs as the main "flower" constituents, perhaps supplemented by a carved wooden spoon or two or an attractively patterned wooden meat mallet. In a living room, pebbles and driftwood might be more appropriate accompaniments, while a flower arrangement for a bathroom could also benefit from the use of sea shells and flowers bedded down in sand.

When buying bunches of dried flowers you will need to consider the sizes and the shapes of the individual flower heads and how they work together in groups as fillers, or as single, featured blooms in arrangements.

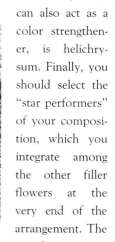

To form the basic shape of an arrangement it is often best to make up tied bunches of flower clusters, such as the spiky shapes of amaranthus, wheat, lavender and larkspur.

Around this basic framework of flowers you can add your fillers. Here you should consider the ever-popular alchemilla mollis (also commonly known as lady's mantle), nigella, poppy heads and achillea. Another popular filler flower, which can also act as a color strengthener, is helichrysum. Finally, you should select the "star performers" of your composition, which you integrate among the other filler flowers at the very end of the arrangement. The idea behind this approach is to create groupings as they would appear in a well-stocked herbaceous border with different heights and combinations of colors. Finishing touches, to pull everything together, could come from dried oak leaves or slices of freeze-dried orange or lemon.

Color
Themes

*t*HE NEUTRAL COLOR THEME IS SO EXTENSIVE THAT THIS CHAPTER COULD EASILY BE EXTENDED TO MAKE UP AN ENTIRE BOOK. ALL OF THE COLORS OF THE PLANTS AND FLOWERS IN THE ARRANGEMENTS THAT FOLLOW ARE ENTIRELY NATURAL — NOTHING HAS BEEN ARTIFI-CIALLY COLORED OR BLEACHED — ALTHOUGH COLORS DO OFTEN LIGHTEN AS PART OF THE DRYING PROCESS. THIS COLOR THEME TAKES IN EVERYTHING FALLING INTO THE CREAM, WHITE, BEIGE AND GRAY SHADES. IN TERMS OF CONTAINERS, IT IS PROBABLY BEST TO OPT FOR THOSE MADE FROM NATURAL MATERIALS — POTS MADE FROM BARK, FOR EXAMPLE, THE SUBDUED SHADES OF EARTHY TERRA COTTA, OR OTHER TYPES OF POTS THAT ARE COVERED WITH LEAVES, MOSS OR CLIPPED CONIFER OR BOX (BUXUS) FOLIAGE.

neutral

The neutral color theme is quite one of the most exciting and satisfying of all, since most of the arrangements you could make in the cream, white, beige and gray color range would be at home in nearly any setting.

In a traditional country cottage – or in a country-influenced apartment or house in town – a neutral-colored arrangement of dried flowers could act as the perfect foil for a collection of brightly decorated spongeware,

slipware, or Delftware pottery. If, on the other hand, your tastes tend to be less flamboyant, imagine that same arrangement used as a center-piece for a dinner table set with the more mellow brown and yellow tones of a stoneware dinner service.

In a contemporary setting, an arrangement of dried flowers com-posed of neutral tones could provide a softening influence on the harsh lines, reflective surfaces and starkly colored woods and surface finishes that tend to predominate today.

Topiary shapes, made out of lichen and differ-ent types of moss work particularly well in the con-text of any type of neutral theme. But don't forget the pot or con-tainer that is used to house such an arrangement – it, too, needs to carry the theme through, either by blending or con-trasting with the flower and plant colors. If symmetry is important, then topiary trees often look at their best when used in pairs, perhaps one either side of a mantlepiece.

You can make lichen trees to any shape and height you want, and you can place them in parts of rooms that

OPPOSITE *The classic beauty of a single-ball lichen topiary tree, which has been constructed around a short stem of betula (silver birch). The cream-colored pot helps to reinforce the color theme.*
ABOVE *Providing strong architectural form, the "star" in this collection of neutrals is a three-tier lichen tree, the stem of which has been neatly wrapped with coils of plain, natural-colored rope.*

19

receive little, if any, natural light or where there are extremes of temperature that would soon kill a growing plant. A simpler idea, but one equally effective, involves covering shaped pieces of florist's foam – oasis balls – with lichen or moss, attaching this material with stub wires or glue. Three of these in a terra cotta pot placed on a window-sill or shelf could form an eye-catching highlight, as would a collection of different-sized moss balls in a wooden or glass bowl used as a table centerpiece.

Another valuable plant in the neutrals collection is wheat. There is a natural affinity between stems of wheat, basically just an ornamental grass, and wickerwork used for old-fashioned baskets. If the wicker is a little loose, you could try working the wheat stems into the weave of the basket and, as a finishing touch, extra ears of wheat can be used as a garland for the rim, glued into place, or as an attractive arrangement covering the handle. This would look ideal in a traditional-style kitchen or

breakfast area in your own home; it would also make the perfect gift for a friend who has recently moved house, with the wheat symbolizing health and prosperity. Fill the center of the basket with fresh green apples to make it a charming as well as a very practical present.

Wheat also lends itself to traditional shield arrangements designed

OPPOSITE *If shelf or table space is tight, then a wall-mounted wheat shield might be the ideal solution. Wheat also lends itself to topiary trees and balls, which can work well with the warmer shades of terra cotta pots.*
BELOW *A rustic fruit container and a spiky ball of wheat looking like a sleeping hedgehog.*

ABOVE *A round basket filled with old terra cotta pots, burlap, bunches of wheat tied with raffia, cloth bags of herbs, garlic cloves, and a few bunches of dried neutrals make up a display for a dresser or sideboard in a kitchen or dining room.*

OPPOSITE *A drop garland, about 3ft (90cm) long, built on a base of dried moss and chicken wire.*

for wall-mounting. Another idea to try is a spiky wheat tree, again using a birch stem as the tree trunk. If this doesn't appeal to you, then what about using wheat bunched together, covering not only the birch stem but also the container as well? Simplest of all, but no less effective in the right setting, is just a plain terra cotta pot filled to overflowing with upright stems of wheat held in place with a piece of florist's foam safely out of sight in the bottom of the container. Leave the pot its natural, warm, earthy color or paint it in cream or off-white if the pot is too new and stark-looking.

"Accessories" to go with a neutral color theme need to be chosen with care so that the overall effect is not diluted. Burlap (hessian) sacking, cut to size and ruffled around the bottom of the stems, is one way of disguising the constructional elements of the arrangement. Raffia ties also look good with neutral colors and sea shells, too, can be used as fillers toward the bottom of a display.

*Y*ELLOW IS PERHAPS THE MOST CHEERFUL OF ALL THE COLOR THEMES. IT IS THE OBVIOUS HUE WE ASSOCIATE WITH SPRING, BRINGING WITH IT THE HOPE OF SUNNIER SKIES AND THE CERTAINTY OF STEADILY LENGTHENING DAYS. IF YOU HAVE A GLOOMY CORNER IN ANY ROOM IN YOUR HOME, OR YOU NEED TO MAKE A DEFINITE COLOR STATEMENT, THEN YELLOW IS ONE OF THE COLORS YOU NEED TO CONSIDER. HOWEVER, YOU CANNOT DIVORCE THE COLOR OF YOUR FLOWER ARRANGEMENT FROM THE OTHER COLORS IN THE ROOM IN WHICH IT WILL BE SEEN. IN THIS REGARD, YELLOW IS QUITE OBLIGING, TONING WELL WITH A RANGE OF GREENS AS WELL AS A NEUTRAL COLOR THEME. IF COLOR CONTRASTS ARE MORE APPEALING, THEN TRY YELLOWS AND BLUES TOGETHER.

yellow

Being such a strong and intense hue, yellow is often best used in single-color displays. A mass of yellow rose heads, for example, in a plain pot of a toning or neutral color can make a positive, eye-catching design statement in the home.

Relying on a single color to carry a display is not as restricting as you might initially think, however. The range of yellows is large indeed, from the strident, sulfurous yellows of flowers such as sunflowers right through the color card to the clear, fresh-seeming spring yellows that you see in many of the narcissi varieties. It is the narcissi that introduce another facet of this color theme, since many have a center that could more properly be described as being orange rather than yellow. It does seem quite reasonable, therefore, to allow into this color theme yellow-orange, burnt orange, salmon, copper, and, of course, the wonderfully rich shades of the golds.

Part of making the best use of a particular color range is developing an instinct for different color associations, which you can then employ

LEFT *A mouth-watering and an aromatic creation – an orange-slice tree on a cinnamon-stick base, housed in an old terra cotta pot topped with a covering of dried moss.*

OPPOSITE *The height of a topiary tree needs to be appropriate in terms of its setting. These two curry cloud trees are built around a contorted willow stem and a betula stem.*

to create a very specific effect. For example, make up a simple hand-held bouquet by bunching together yellow and blue flower heads and note the ways the colors interact with each other. Don't bother trimming the stems to size, for this is simply an exercise in color association. To this bouquet, next add a few examples of an intense red flower color and watch the combination really start to sing out at you. You should certainly experiment in this fashion with

ABOVE *An unsual wattle hurdle decorated with terra cotta pots, generous bunches of wheat and individual arrangements of dried herbs and roses.*

OPPOSITE *A wall garland of eucalyptus and driftwood, with cream and yellow dried roses.*

flower colors in the florist's shop or your specialist dried-flower supplier before selecting the particular blooms you wish to buy.

One of the currently popular dried flowers favored by arrangers is commonly known as the yellow curry flower. It has an attractive, fluffy flower head and is usually used in bunches, with the stems trimmed to length and then wired or tied together so that the heads form dense clusters. You can also use them as you would moss – to carpet any pre-formed shape, creating mounds of not only spectacular color but also valuable textural interest. They are quite economical to use in this way, in fact, since once you have wired them up they cover quite a large area.

Yellow flowers used as single blooms can often be regarded as "star performers" in a mixed-color composition, especially the longer-stemmed varieties. Other yellow flowers worth considering are the spray yellow marigolds and also the ever-cheerful daffodils, which have

ABOVE *Yellow has been used to visually link the different elements of this arrangement.*

OPPOSITE *A curry tree, with clouds of flowers molded around a contorted salix branch, held upright in its pot with quick-drying plaster.*

been dried in a mixture of sand and silica gel. They give an arrangement a real boost.

Using a predominantly yellow flower arrangement in a house with dark-stained wooden walls or a somber color scheme can help to provide a much-needed feeling of welcome and warmth. It also works in places that receive little in the way of natural light. Try such an arrangement on a hallway table, for example, where it will be the first thing visitors see on entering your home. You can create even more impact if you echo the shapes and colors of plants growing outside in the garden in your arrangement – this is an excellent way of integrating "inside" and "outside" for a real feeling of cultivated continuity.

As a novel idea for a container , try gluing preserved magnolia leaves around the outside of a basket and filling the center with masses of yellow roses. Simple ideas such as this, using one or two basic ingredients, often work best.

*V*IBRANT, RICH AND EYE-CATCHING ARE SOME OF THE TERMS THAT CAN BE APPLIED TO THE RED COLOR THEME. JUST LOOK AT THE INTENSITY OF THE COLOR OF THE URN OF ROSES ON THE LEFT AND YOU WILL SEE HOW DIFFERENT DRIED FLOWERS ARE TODAY FROM THE OLD "DUST COLLECTORS" OF THE PAST. THE YELLOW AND PINK ARRANGEMENTS HAVE BEEN INCLUDED TO DEMONSTRATE HOW THESE HUES CAN ACT AS VALUABLE COMPLEMENTS IF YOU ARE USING RED AS A SINGLE-COLOR ARRANGEMENT. LIKE YELLOW, YOU CAN USE RED TO BRIGHTEN UP A DARK CORNER OF A ROOM, AND IT WORKS PARTICULARLY WELL WHEN SEEN AGAINST WOODS SUCH AS MAHOGANY AND OAK. ON A FESTIVE NOTE, REDS ARE OFTEN USED AT CHRISTMAS, MIXED WITH EVERGREENS AND DRIED FRUITS.

red

There is always something uplifting about a display of dried red flowers, and if used in a mixed-color display, then red also tends to add a little drama and a lot of color depth. Red roses, in particular, are closely associated with love and romance. For that special person in your life, can you think of a better present to give than an old, mellow terra cotta pot filled with dried rosebuds as a Valentine's Day offering?

One of the advantages of using predominantly red-colored arrangements is that they seem to work so well in almost any type and style of home – from a traditional cottage, full of rough plaster walls, beamed ceilings and time-worn wooden furniture, right through to more contemporary settings such as conversions on mills or

barns, with their sharp, well-defined lines, their large interior spaces and hard surfaces of stone or brick.

Try making up some terra cotta pots of dried red roses and placing them in different positions about your home. How you then light them is critical if you are to maximize their full dramatic qualities. They could look superb, for example, if they are indirectly lit by lamps on small side-tables, or "spotlit" by very directional natural light, entering from a side window, so that they are seen against a densely shadowed, featureless background. For a completely integrated, thoughtful display, take the time to trim the individual stems so that the heights of the flowers suit that of the lampshade and look in the correct

OPPOSITE *A triple-cone toleware container filled with an attractive assortment of dried-flower specimens. This container can also be used for a display of fresh flowers.*

ABOVE *A matched pair of red rose trees in plain terra cotta pots, lit naturally by window light, together with a simple arrangement of loose dried red roses.*

proportion in relation to the other items nearby – such as old candlesticks, a china jug, or any other ornament you may be using in a supporting type of role.

Another dramatically red flower to consider is the wonderful celosia, also known as cockscomb, which you can use to make topiary trees. It has such an interesting form, and the color can be so rich and intense, that it is sometime difficult to remember that it really is a natural, undyed product. You can also use celosia as a filler in the base of a large arrangement, or even wired together in clusters in the form of a garland.

If you find the cost of buying some dried flowers a little on the high side, especially items such as red or pink roses, then bear in mind that a typical arrangement lasts between three and four years, if care is taken. At the end of this time you may well want a new arrangement for your room. If so, carefully take the old one apart and, using a hair dryer set to low power and a cool setting, blow the dust off any of the flowers you are reserving for reuse. This will help to revive their colour. Discard any flowers that have faded badly. Then all you need do is start again with a selection of fresh specimens.

OPPOSITE *A mixed collection of dried red flowers and poppy seed heads wired onto an interestingly twisted old ivy stem.*
BELOW *The depth of color of this single-ball celosia tree naturally draws attention and creates a focal point for any part of a room.*

*t*HERE IS A GOOD SELECTION OF DIFFERENT SHADES OF BLUE TO BE FOUND IN DRIED FLOWERS, RANGING FROM PALE GRAY-BLUES RIGHT THE WAY THROUGH TO VIBRANT PURPLES. MORE THAN ALL THE OTHER COLOR THEMES, THE BLUE RANGE OF DRIED FLOWERS MOST NEEDS TO BE USED IN A MONOCHROMATIC WAY. THE ONLY REAL PROBLEM YOU MIGHT FIND WITH THE BLUE THEME IS IN POSITIONING YOUR ARRANGEMENT. BLUE SEEMS TO SOAK UP LIGHT LIKE A SPONGE, SO YOU MAY FIND THAT A BLUE ARRANGEMENT SET IN A DARK POSITION OR SEEN AGAINST DARK BACKGROUND COLORS CREATES A SORT OF DEAD SPOT IN A ROOM. HOWEVER, IN A BRIGHT, WELL-LIT ENVIRONMENT, THE "COOLNESS" OF A BLUE FLORAL DISPLAY CAN PROVIDE A VALUABLE DECORATIVE CONTRAST.

blue

RIGHT *A double-ended wall shield made of fragrant eucalyptus branches. A raffia tie gives the shield a "waist" and a convenient fixing point.*

OPPOSITE *A delicate lavender cloud tree using a contorted piece of willow as its support. The blue and white container and curtain fabric set it off beautifully.*

Perhaps the only color that readily associates with the blue color range of dried flowers is white, which can help to lift a predominantly blue arrangement out and away from a darkish setting. This two-color scheme can look particularly stylish set against blue and white fabrics of the right tones, and it could also look perfect if seen on a country-style kitchen dresser overflowing with the type of blue and white china often described as Delftware.

Of all the blues, lavender is by far and away the flower most widely used by arrangers. Not only does lavender come in different shades and intensities of blue, its spiky, up-right form makes it valuable as part of the structural framework of an arrangement, and, as an additional bonus, lavender is beautifully fragrant. As a simple display, fill two or three blue and white ginger jars with bunches of spiky lavender heads, each secured with plaited ties of natural raffia. Or for more vibrancy and elegance, combine lavender with purple statice.

For a more ambitious display, consider how lovely a "cloud tree" could look, made from a mixture of different blue flower heads. The "trunk" for a tree such as this would

fragrant. Although not a flower at
all, a marvellous foliage filler, and
well worth noting here, is the blue-
tinged eucalyptus. Stems of these
leaves give an arrangement height
and lend it a sculptural form. If used
as an ornamental, eucalyptus is heav-
ily pruned every year. This not only
keeps it small, but also ensures that
the new growth produces leaves with
a neat, rounded shape. If left un-
pruned, a eucalyptus would soon
attain great height and develop char-
acteristically strap-like leaves, which
can be attractive in their own right.

The fragrance of the blue flower
range makes them particularly suitable as air fresheners in a bathroom
setting, or as providers of soft scents
to lull you gently to sleep in your
bedroom. Both lavender and eucalyptus complement each other when
used in association with gray lichen
moss and sea shells. An elegant
choice of container for an arrangement such as this would be a glass
bowl. Or, for a more robust display,
you might fill three different-sized

usually be provided by contorted
stems of willow or hazel. It is onto
these stems that you attach prepared
cloud-shaped wired constructions of
moss and blue flower heads. If you
like the idea, you can try to copy the
spectacular examples of living design
that the best of the bonsai growers
achieve in their diminutive trees.

As well as lavender, many other
dried flowers in the blue range are

OPPOSITE *A single-head marjoram tree supported on a twig "trunk" arranged in a moss-topped terra cotta pot.*
RIGHT *A large-leaved ball-topiary tree made from eucalyptus. The gray lichen moss used around the tree trunk not only hides the constructional elements of the design, it also helps to unify the colorings of the plant and its container.*

terra cotta pots with lavender heads, all trimmed to the same length and tied off neatly with garden string, and place them in descending order of size on a sunny window-sill. Another fragrant idea is to strip lavender flowers off their spikes and fill some pretty cotton sachets with them. Hidden in a drawer, they will impart their scent to all your clothes.

The darker shades of blue lend themselves more to strong design themes than do the lighter shades. For an architectural type of arrangement, imagine criss-cross patterns of bunches of deep blue flower heads – such as cornflowers – in a wall garland, together with poppy seed heads, driftwood, eucalyptus and cream-colored roses. If a classic approach is to be preferred, place stalks of delphinium flowers in a glass cylinder filled with different shades of blue- and neutral-colored pot-pourri ingredients. Another blue flower that works exceptionally well when seen massed together is the blue hydrangea, perhaps placed in a log basket to fill a fireplace not being used during the summer months.

Another way to fill an unused fireplace is to make an appropriately sized wall shield from lavender stalks attached to a wooden frame. Smaller versions look good in pairs, one used either side of a mirror. To make a lavender shield, first bunch the flower heads together and wire them into a moss ball. Next, wire the flower stems you would normally discard into the ball to make the fan-shaped bottom part of the arrangement. The finished shield looks like an old-fashioned corn stook.

If you have a terra cotta pot you have not yet found a use for, fill it with lavender, then edge it with a frieze of red or yellow roses, depending on your color scheme, and finish it with a tie of raffia.

ABOVE *A lavender wall shield. The same design can be used with wheat as the subject.*
LEFT *Terra cotta pots filled with lavender and edged with red roses.*

Wreaths

*W*REATHS ARE USED THROUGHOUT THE WORLD
ON ALL MANNER OF OCCASIONS. WHETHER MADE OF
FRESH FLOWERS FOR A FUNERAL OR OUT OF DRIED
FLOWERS FOR A LONG-LASTING WALL-HUNG
DECORATION, THE WREATH HAS BEEN IN USE FOR
HUNDREDS OF YEARS. WREATHS LEND THEMSELVES
VERY HAPPILY TO FESTIVE MOMENTS TOO. WE HAVE
ALL SEEN WREATHS IN CELEBRATION OF CHRISTMAS,
HUNG ON THE OUTSIDE OF A DOOR OR USED AS A
TABLE CENTERPIECE FOR CHRISTMAS DINNER. THESE
CAN BE QUITE SIMPLY MADE FROM FIR TWIGS BENT
AROUND A PRE-FORMED CIRCULAR FRAME AND WIRED
INTO POSITION. THIS CAN THEN BE DECORATED WITH
SEASONAL FANCIES, SUCH AS FIR CONES AND COLORFUL
CLUSTERS OF DRIED FRUITS.

wreaths

If you have a blank wall somewhere in your home, perhaps one you are planning to fill at some later stage with a mirror or a special painting, a simple wreath could look superb as an interim "hole-filler". It is more than likely, though, that even when you have hung your mirror or painting, you will not want to discard the wreath, and so you will find it a spot in some other part of your home.

Although wall- or door-hung celebration wreaths are what the majority of us most readily associate with this type of dried-flower arrangement, wreaths can be just as effective if used flat on a suitable surface. Add a candle, held securely in place in a special holder, and place a clear-glass storm lantern over the flame, and you could have a festive light for a mantelpiece or table setting.

In terms of design, when making a wreath out of dried flowers always remember to group your different varieties of flowers in good-sized, bold clumps. This is the only way your wreath will take on a really striking appearance once finished. It is often best to start working the spiky types of flowers into the wreath first to help define its overall shape and character. For this, you could consider the flamboyant, tassel-forming amaranthus flowers. Next come the fillers, such as the arching stems of alchemilla, helichrysum, and the attractive, purple-pink flowers of origanum. And finally, you will want to add your "star performers". In this role, look at the lovely achillea and clusters of dahlias.

RIGHT *A wreath made of mixed dried herbs, ideal for a traditional kitchen, together with a matching pot-pourri basket beneath.*

OPPOSITE *This charming burlap-based wreath would be ideal for a harvest festival. It is decorated with terra cotta pots and herb sachets.*

What would seem to be the most difficult part of making a wreath – forming the circular shape itself – in fact is the easiest. Any good florist or dried-flower supplier will always carry a stock of wreath frames in different sizes and shapes. A heart-shaped frame, for example, could be the perfect starting point for a romantic Valentine's Day wreath, or a horseshoe-shaped frame could be made into a personalized good-luck gift for somebody you know with college examinations looming.

Whatever frame you decide on, you will normally disguise the wire frame with a good covering of moss. The secret here is to make very certain that the moss you use has thoroughly dried out. Any moisture left in the moss will very quickly cause your flowers to spoil.

If you want to avoid using moss altogether, you can always wrap the frame in burlap. This material is very easy to penetrate with the stub wires used to attach the decorative surface elements. Seen against a burlap background, clusters of small terra cotta pots, together with sachets of dried herbs, could look particularly appropriate if used in a wreath designed for a country-style kitchen.

Of all the festive occasions, it is Christmas that generates the most interest in wreath making. One more unusual idea you might like to try involves weaving the strikingly colored branches of the red cornus (dogwood) into the wreath frame so that the wire is completely hidden. The stems of the cornus are very flexible, so this should not be a problem. Onto this background, attach further bundles of twigs, together with clusters of amaranthus, celosia, and groups of single and spray red roses. You could also wire walnuts, chestnuts and Brazil nuts, each in their own nest made of moss, onto the wreath, and, as a finishing touch, glue pecan and hazelnuts together to make a gloriously nutty seasonal offering.

When selecting the individual flowers, bunches of flowers, cones, cinnamon sticks, nuts, and so on, you will find that odd numbers, such as 3s, 5s, and 7s, are in nearly all cases easier to design with than even numbers of items.

RIGHT *By restricting your choice of colors for a wreath to just one of the major color themes – here red – you can create a dried-flower arrangement with real dramatic impact. This richly colored wreath uses red amaranthus, pink larkspur and pink helichrysum together with pink and red roses and dark red heads of peonies.*

Scents

*I*F YOU ENJOY THE HEADY SCENTS OF FLOWERS IN YOUR HOME ALL THE YEAR AROUND, THEN AN ATTRACTIVE POT-POURRI BASKET IS THE IDEAL SOLUTION. POT-POURRI IS A LOOSE MIXTURE OF DRIED PETALS AND FLOWER HEADS WHICH MAY BE USED IN MANY DIFFERENT WAYS. YOU COULD, FOR EXAMPLE, FOLLOW THE ILLUSTRATION ON PAGE 51, WHICH SHOWS A WREATH AND MATCHING POT-POURRI BASKET ALREADY MADE UP. FLORISTS AND SPECIALIST SUPPLIERS ALWAYS STOCK A WIDE RANGE OF POT-POURRI INGREDIENTS — SIMPLY CHOOSE THE COLORS AND SCENTS THAT MOST APPEAL TO YOU. ALTHOUGH LONG-LASTING, YOU MAY NEED TO RENEW THE MIXTURE ONCE OR TWICE A YEAR IN ORDER TO KEEP YOUR POT-POURRI AT ITS MOST FRAGRANT.

scents

One of the most creative and attractive ways of displaying pot-pourri is in the context of garlanded baskets, although, in some settings simply mixing your ingredients together in a

plain glass bowl or on a wooden platter can be very effective, too.

One design that has proved to be very popular over the years involves weaving a garland of rose heads and assorted sea shells around the rim of a basket, and then filling the middle with rose petals of the appropriate color for the room in which the basket will be displayed.

As well as color, you also need to consider what type and style of decoration will suit each individual room. For example, if your pot-pourri basket is to be used in the kitchen, you could add a selection of red beans, apples and pears, grouped together in clusters. The hallway is another favorite place for a pot-pourri basket. If placed on an occasional table, perhaps near the bottom of the stairs, the fragrance will greet your visitors when they enter as well as waft upstairs to add a delicate hint of scent to the bedrooms. In winter, there is something very special about coming inside from the cold to be met by the delightful fresh smell of

OPPOSITE ABOVE *An informal and attractive yellow and green basket of fragrant pot-pourri, lined with burlap and then filled with a nutty selection of ingredients to give form and texture.*

OPPOSITE BELOW *The rustic charm of this pot-pourri basket edged with clusters of lichen and bunches of lavender would look perfect in a country cottage setting.*

ABOVE *A mixed blue and red decorated basket, filled with a mixture of red rose pot-pourri.*

lavender rising from a pot-pourri basket placed on a radiator cover (the heat from the radiator increases the fragrance to quite a degree).

Pot-pourri in baskets can also be used in a seasonal or festive fashion, with the decorations and accessories specifically targeted to suit the occasion. At Christmas time, for example, it can be a wonderful idea to garland baskets with a wide selection of vividly colored pot-pourri ingredients in the red and pink shades, and then tie a bow in beautiful velvet around the handle. Next, fill your Christmas basket with your colorful pot-pourri to which you have added such chunky ingredients as pieces of

ABOVE *An interesting collection of apple- and pear-shaped bean-ball fruits.*

OPPOSITE *An assortment of balls, covered in shells and red beans for texture and shape and aniseed, cloves, and roses for fragrance.*

bark, whole fir cones, aniseed stars (available at good craft stores), nutmeg and small cinnamon sticks. To these ingredients you can then mix in tiny amounts of essential oils to produce just the right fragrance.

Another traditional way of introducing both color and scent into specific parts of your home, although not a pot-pourri idea, is to make up a scented pomander. One design for a pomander that most people are familiar with is to cover the outside of an orange so densely with cloves that the skin can hardly be seen at all. But you can cover any base shape with the ingredients that most appeal to you and that best suit its position in the home.

index

The author would like to thank:
Sylvia and Les Lucy
Chrissie and Howard Sage
Chrissie Rouffignac